So, You're Moving to Philly!

A Handbook to Being a Philadelphian

RUSSELL C WORDS

SO YOU'RE MOVING TO PHILADELPHIA:
A HANDBOOK TO BEING A PHILADELPHIAN

Copyright 2014 by Russell C Words

Russell C Words
Flat Rock NC 28739

International Standard Book Number 978-1-935771-27-2

Manufactured in the United States of America

Moving to Philadelphia...

Prologue

So you are thinking of moving to Philadelphia. Or are moving or are already here.

Some eight million Americans move to a new state every year. Now you're one of them. You've come to right place.

With the essays in these pages you'll learn the explanations behind the quirks, the traditions and the secrets that make Philadelphia uniquely Philadelphia. *So You're Moving to Philadelphia!...A Handbook to Being a Philadelphian* will help you join the club in no time.

Missing signs for the Blue Route? Solved. The valley of the Delaware Valley? A mystery no more. Murals? Mummers? Main Line? Sorted out. Identified. Revealed. Cars parked in the middle of the street? Well, not everything has an explanation.

Celebrating in Philadelphia...Cheering in Philadelphia... Driving in Philadelphia...Eating in Philadelphia...Exploring in Philadelphia...Playing in Philadelphia...Politicking in Philadelphia. This book will have you speaking like a native in no time.

Because the next best thing to being a native Philadelphian is being able to pass as one.

What's Up With...

those things that make
Philadelphia uniquely Philadelphia

What's Up With...the Delaware Valley?

When you arrive in Philadelphia you will hear the term "Delaware Valley" bandied about for your new residence as much, if not more, than "Philadelphia." If you look on a map you will find no "Delaware Valley." If you go exploring you will find no verdant hillsides surrounding a sylvan waterway. What is this cryptic place of which you speak?

The Delaware Valley is media shorthand for the entire Philadelphia metropolitan area. So Philadelphia is really not just the city but 15 - 15! - surrounding counties in Pennsylvania, New Jersey, Delaware and even Maryland. You are now part of a pulsating, growing population of more than six million that is the fourth largest metropolitan market in America, not just one of Philadelphia's 1.5 million residents, a total that has dropped by over half a million from 1950. Today you can live more than 50 miles from where William Penn laid out the street plan for his City of Brotherly Love in 1682 and still call yourself a "Philadelphian."

What's Up With...All the Multisyllabic Place Names?

Passyunk, Moyamensing, Cohocksink, Aramingo, Manayunk, Schuylkill, Wissahickon, Conshohocken. Philadelphia is loaded with exotic-sounding place names. They are a legacy of the Lenni Lenape Indians who fished and farmed the Delaware Valley for 10,000 years before the coming of European settlers. Upon arriving in 1682 to claim the land given to him by King Charles II to repay a debt owed his father, William Penn famously negotiated a treaty with the Lenni Lenape on the banks of the Delaware River in what is today the City's Fishtown neighborhood. As he set up his "New Wales" colony Penn

retained many of the Lenape names for townships. But when it came to naming his dream town Penn turned not to native languages but to classic Greek - Philadelphia literally means "The City of Brotherly Love."

Penn earned a reputation for fair dealings with the Lenni Lenape but after he died in 1781 his heirs were not so benevolent. More and more Lenape land was sold off for profit and most of the first settlers were forced to move west until the tribe exists today mostly in Oklahoma. The Lenape Nation of Pennsylvania, however, still numbers about 300 people while continuing to live in their ancestral homeland in the Delaware Valley.

What's Up With... The Quakers

Following the English Civil War in the mid-1600s dissatisfied Christian splinter groups began to emerge. George Fox, the son of a weaver, was one such religious rebel. Convinced that it was possible to have a direct relationship with the Lord without the benefit of clergy, he traveled far and wide with his controversial message before being hauled in front of a magistrate in 1650 on charges of blasphemy. When Fox railed against the judges to "tremble at the word of the Lord" he was ridiculed as a "quaker." And so members of the Religious Society of Friends have been called ever since.

Fox was imprisoned and despite persecution for their unpopular theological challenges and pacifist ways the number of Friends grew to more than 60,000 by 1680. By that time Fox had been in and out of prison and traveled to America to establish the Quaker movement in the British colonies. However there were only two places in the New World where it turned out Quakers were not routinely persecuted - Rhode Island and, after a staunch Fox ally named William Penn arrived to claim his inheritance, Pennsylvania.

Quakers have no written creed or fixed tenets of belief and no defined program of prayer. Congregants enter a typically unadorned meeting room and sit in silence, perhaps speaking aloud if the spirit

moves them. You can experience meetinghouses across the Delaware Valley, including the Arch Street Meeting House that is the oldest still in use in Philadelphia and the largest in the world. Penn donated the land to be used as a burial ground in 1701. The long, center-pedimented brick building was begun in 1803 with the wings added in 1811.

The Friends eventually migrated west, settling in pockets of like-minded communities across the country. But after more than 300 years it is still Philadelphia that is most associated with the Quak-

ers. The University of Pennsylvania, even though it is not a Quaker school, has adopted the Quaker as its mascot. The nickname was actually hung on the school's sports teams by newspaper writers in the 1880s and it just stuck. There have been two Quaker Presidents - Herbert Hoover and Richard Nixon. Nixon's ancestral roots are in the Delaware Valley; his kin, Quaker ministers, settled in Darby outside of Philadelphia in the early 1700s.

What's Up With...the Statue of William Penn on Top of City Hall?

When planning began on City Hall in 1871 it was intended to be the tallest building in the world but when it was finally finished 30 years - and eight mayors - later, City Hall was surpassed by both the Eiffel Tower and the Washington Monument. Instead, city boosters hung "Billy Penn's hat" on the fact that at 547 feet it was the world's

tallest habitable building, a title it held for less than a decade. Today, it remains the tallest masonry building ever constructed. City Hall is topped by a 37-foot, 27-ton bronze statue of city founder William Penn, one of 250 sculptures created by Alexander Milne Calder that adorn the building inside and out. The statue is the tallest atop any building in the world.

By "gentleman's agreement" no building was constructed that Billy Penn could not look over in Philadelphia for more than 80 years. Compared to other major cities, the lack of skyscrapers gave Philly a personal scale that it kept all the way until 1987 when One Liberty Place shattered the unoffical pact and soared almost 400 feet above Penn's hat. So much for that tradition.

Penn's statue is hollow and a narrow access tunnel inside leads to a small, 22-inch-diameter hatch atop the hat. It is not open to the public but an elevator can take you up to an observation deck just below the statue for the best views in the City. Even if it is blocked by a few super high-rises.

What's Up With... Yo?

"Yo, what accent?" There is a perception of Philadelphians wielding a distinctive accent but you'll be hard-pressed to tell the natives from the transplants when you get here. Except for a few classic give-away words such as : "wooder" for water, "beyoodeeful" for beautiful, "tal" for towel and, of course, "Iggles" for the much-beloved hometown football team.

Most of America's impression of the Philadelphia dialect is tied to Rocky Balboa, the fictional pugilist portrayed by Sylvester Stallone for three decades and six movies. His "Yo, Adrian" has become the go-to example of Philadelphia-speak. The attention-grabbing "yo" was popularized by many Italian-American youths in the mid-1900s but has been linked almost exclusively with Philadelphia. The word "yo," by the way appears in the dictionary but will not be accepted by Scrabble. Play it with a fellow Philadelphian, however, and you will never get a challenge.

What's Up With... Wawa?

"It's the convenience store of the gods," lamented one former devotee who had recently moved just beyond the reach of Wawa food market stores.

It was back in 1892 that George Wood moved from the Maurice River in New Jersey to the rolling hills of Delaware County to start a dairy farm. Wood built his herd from cows that had sailed across the Atlantic Ocean from the British Island of Guernsey. He called his operation "Wawa" after his new hometown; its name derives from the Ojibwe Indian word for "Canadian goose." The wild Canadian goose in flight was recruited as the company logo.

The Wood family sold milk until people stopped relying on glass bottles delivered to their doorstep in the 1960s. In 1964 the family opened its first food market on MacDade Boulevard in Folsom. That was some 600 stores and countless millions of paper cups of coffee ago. Wawa serves well over 100 million cups of coffee every year - it is the 8th largest seller of coffee in America behind only national chains with names like Starbucks, McDonalds and Dunkin' Donuts. All that coffee helps wash down the 80 million Shorti hoagies and other sandwiches it sells each year.

Wawa did not start selling gasoline at its stores until 1996. Today one percent of all the gas in America is pumped at a Wawa. That same year Wawa began its now-famous program of no usage fees at its in-store ATMs - a convenience that customers have taken advantage of more than one billion times. Yes, Wawa has saved its customers more than $1 billion in bank fees. No wonder Wawa has over one million "likes" on its Facebook page.

It will not be long after you move to Philly before you find yourself in a Wawa. You may even come face-to-beak with Wally, the Wawa goose mascot, who is kept busy officiating over individual store milestones. Wawa may be without peer as a convenience store but it is not without competition. 7-Eleven is still in the market and Turkey Hill of Lancaster County, with its super-creamy ice cream, offers gas station-food stores in the western suburbs.

Also in the western suburbs Altoona-based Sheetz has begun opening stores. Sheetz, with its flashy red stores, is to Western Pennsylvania what Wawa is to Philadelphia. One thing Pennsylvania seems to have perfected is the convenience store. As the two chains have both expanded southwards they are bumping into each other's territories. Partisans are lining up; battle lines are being drawn. The convenience store wars have even caught the attention of the *Washington Post* and the *New York Times*. Remember, you're in Philadelphia now - the right choice is Wawa.

What's Up With...All the Cars Parked in the Middle of the Street?

You will see them there at any time of the day, lined up with impunity in the middle of South Broad Street. Supposedly it is illegal to park a car in the middle of the street but no tickets are ever handed out. Why that is so and how the practice began is one of the enduring mysteries in Philadelphia.

It has been going on for so long there are as many theories as cars rolled up onto medians. Some say center-of-the-street parking began a century ago when Broad Street was lined with funeral homes and the police gave mourners a pass on illegal parking. Others just point to the thousands of row houses without garages and a paucity of legal spaces. But there are no answers, it just is.

So when you're in South Philadelphia, give it a try. After all, there is no faster way to earning your Philadelphia bonafides than fighting a parking ticket in traffic court.

What's Up With...All the Trolleys?

San Francisco's cable cars get all the fawning love for quaint intracity mass transit but Philly's fleet of antique trolley cars deserve a shout out as well. Just about every major American city has torn up its streetcar system over the years. Philadelphia was busy ripping down as well. There were once 4,000 trolleys on 65 lines across the city. But SEPTA (Southeast Pennsylvania Transportation Authority) stopped short of complete destruction. Five street-level and subway lines still operate in the city and out to select suburban towns on almost twenty miles of track. The trolley cars run down the center of city streets with passengers boarding from stations perched precariously in narrow medians.

In 2005 SEPTA plowed $100 million into opening another trolley line along Girard Avenue beside Fairmount Park; the line dated back to 1859 when it was served by horse-pulled cars. You can now ride SEPTA Route 15 on circa 1947 Deco-style trolley cars that were rebuilt from the wheels up to the tune of $1.3 million per car.

What's Up With...the Mummers?

Only a handful of parades have a national reputation - Mardi Gras in New Orleans, the Macy's Thanksgiving Parade in New York City, the Rose Parade in Pasadena...and the Mummers Parade on New Year's Day in Philadelphia.

Mummers date back to antiquity, costumed entertainers who danced in the New Year during fanciful festivals. The Old World traditions, however, were ignored almost everywhere in America save for Philadelphia. Mummery was recorded on the banks of the Delaware River with the original Swedish settlers in the 1600s. By the 1800s end-of-year revelers had loosely organized into groups who would travel through Philadelphia neighborhoods singing songs and dancing in accompaniment to discharging firearms.

The City organized the first official Mummers Parade on January 1, 1901. Over the years costumes became more and more outlandish - especially in the depiction of women who were not allowed to join in the merriment until the 1970s - and clubs staged fundraising events throughout the year to finance participation.

The parade today includes over 10,000 marchers competing in four divisions: Comic, Fancy, Fancy Brigade and String Band. Many of the celebrants labor under costumes weighing 100 pounds or more; a captain's costume alone can cost $10,000. Weather is always a concern leading up to the Mummers Parade with windy conditions being more of a concern than cold due to the costumes. In addition the parade fans can watch the Fancy Brigades practice and put the finishing touches on props during the Mummer Fest at the Pennsylvania Convention Center in the days leading up to the New Year.

What's Up With...the Main Line?

Start listing those area's in America oozing "old money" and it never takes long to get to Philadelphia's Main Line. Hollywood cemented the Main Line's cachet in 1940 with the romantic comedy, the *Philadelphia Story* featuring the socialite hijinks of Cary Grant, Katharine Hepburn and Jimmy Stewart.

Back in the 1800s there actually was a "main line" - the tracks built by the Pennsylvania Railroad heading west out of Philadelphia to Lancaster and Harrisburg and eventually all the way to Chicago. The railroad owned most of the land surrounding its tracks and to encourage development it built way stations two minutes apart from Overbrook in the city out to Paoli in Chester County.

It was not a hard sell to lure wealthy Philadelphians out of the city in the 1800s. Thick smoke from factories choked the skies and horses and rooting pigs fouled the streets making humid summers particularly unbearable. Large country estates were favored as much for the "healthy living" as they were for their status. The tiny stations developed into now-familiar towns with names like Wynnewood, Villanova, Gladwyne and Ardmore. Some of the country's most famous private schools - Bryn Mawr, Rosemont, Haverford - were founded to serve the tony new communities. And the residents gathered in some of America's most exclusive clubs - Merion Cricket Club, Gulph Mills Club, the Philadelphia Country Club.

As you can imagine, there are plenty of towns looking to join the "Main Line." Today just about any affluent town in Philadelphia's western suburbs will try to squeeze under the Main Line umbrella, especially in real estate listings. That includes such towns as Media (Route 1), Newtown Square (Route 3) and Valley Forge (I-76). But the core of the Main Line remains the original towns born of money along Lancaster Pike (Route 30) and the old Pennsylvania Railroad.

What's Up With...All the Murals?

Back in 1984 the City of Philadelphia was waging a losing battle in the war on grafitti. A young muralist named Jane Golden was hired to channel the talents of the city's young street artists into more productive projects. In the three decades the Mural Arts Program under Golden has shepherded over 3,600 murals into existence and engaged thousands of at-risk youths with art education programs.

Philadelphia has more murals than any city in America. In the process the public art has moved well beyond the purview of abandoned brick warehouses. At the Philadelphia International Airport the Mural Arts Program has transformed its parking garage with an 85,000-square foot mural called *How Philly Moves* that shimmers with kinetic energy when viewed from I-95 at, theoretically, 55 miles per hour.

Living in Philadelphia

Celebrating in Philadelphia

Philadelphia Flower Show
Philadelphia Convention Center
March

Nothing juices Philadelphians for the coming of spring like the Philadelphia Flower Show. It all began back in 1829 when 25 members of the then two-year old Pennsylvania Horticultural Society displayed fruits, vegetables, exotic plants and flowers in a tiny Masonic Hall that wouldn't hold a modern high school basketball court. Today the Flower Show is not only the oldest horticultural exhibition in the United States, it is the world's largest indoor plant-based extravaganza, spreading across 33 acres in the Pennsylvania Convention Center. Each year brings a different theme, insuring the 250,000 people that visit over its nine-day run always see something fresh.

Devon Horse Show and Country Fair
Devon
May/June

When the Main Line was new and the roads were still populated by horse-drawn surrys, a group of fox hunters got together to debate the need for better horses. In less than two months the first Devon Horse Show was underway to advance horsemanship and breeding. That was in 1896. By 1914 the Devon Horse Show was the biggest outdoor horse show in the United States and a century later it is still the country's largest equine showcase.

In 1919 a Country Fair was added to benefit Bryn Mawr Hospital. But the event in the shadow of the rambling, long burned-away Devon Inn remained exclusively the purview of the high society horse set until the 1950s when the general public was courted to attend the week-long festival. The elite family trackside boxes and manicured barns remain but as many people come for the flea markets and midway rides as the horses these days.

Don't leave the fabled grounds without indulging in the ultimate Devon Horse Show tradition - the Lemon Stick. This quintessential summer treat is a porous lemon-flavored candy straw jabbed into a lemon to deliver a burst of sweet/tart juice. Philadelphians and Baltimoreans (they use a peppermint stick down in Charm City) go back and forth over which town invented the tangy confection but what is known is that Lemon Sticks were served in the Blue Room on the Devon fairgrounds in the 1920s during Prohibition. In the Blue Room though it wasn't juice being sucked out of the lemons. It was vodka.

Philly Beer Week
various locales
June

As a gateway to so many German immigrants it is no headline-maker that Philadelphia has a rich beer-soaked heritage. But even without a Bavarian background brewing would have played a big role in the town's past since the water was often undrinkable. In the 19th century Philadelphia was hands-down the greatest brewing city in America. The first large-scale lager brewery in the country opened on St. John Street in 1844. Some estimates placed the number of breweries in the City at more than 700; one section of Philly, still surviving, was named Brewerytown.

Prohibition in 1920 put an end to all that. By the time the beer started to flow legally again in the 1930s most beer production had shuffled off to the Midwest. Today, though, the neighborhood breweries are back and since 2008 the City has staged the largest beer celebration of its kind in America with a week of pub crawls, tasting tours and brewing demonstrations. The "Hammer of Glory" travels relay-style through the town on Opening Day of Philly Beer Week, headed for its sober duty to crack open the first keg at Opening Tap and unleash some 600 events.

Manayunk Arts Festival
June

By the middle of the 1800s Philadelphia had become nearly ungovernable. The immigrant population was growing but mostly in the outlying towns and districts of Philadelphia County, none of which was ever in a hurry to enforce the city's laws. It was a common ploy to commit a crime in Philly and then skip across the city line to safety.

That all changed with the Act of Consolidation in 1854 that dissolved the governments of the county's townships, districts and boroughs and folded them into the City of Philadelphia. Most of the new neighborhoods maintained their old identities and that was the case with Manayunk, a hilly manufacturing town on the banks of the Schuylkill River.

The factory jobs drifted away over the years and the commercial district was peppered with abandoned buildings. Manayunk staged a comeback in the 1990s on the strength of its small-town Victorian charm. About the same time the Town began celebrating its infusion of artists with the Manayunk Arts Fest. Today the two-day festival is the largest outdoor arts gathering in the Delaware Valley, attracting more than 300 artists and craftspeople from across the United States and Canada.

Welcome America
various locales
July 4 Week

You would expect the home of the Liberty Bell and Independence Hall to do something BIG on July 4. Then again the Liberty Bell was ignored for years before it was eventually sent on trips around the country as a symbol of independence and the Pennsylvania State House once hosted the city's dog pound in the basement before it was restored in 1950 and immortalized as Independence Hall. Valley Forge was forgotten and overgrown for 100 years. But those neglectful days are long in the past; nowadays Philadelphia never misses a chance to promote itself as the Birthplace of America.

It was up to a professor from Wabash College in Indiana to put the bug in Philadelphia's ear about celebrating the signing of the Declaration of Independence. John L. Campbell had the idea in 1866

that ten years hence the City of Philadelphia might do well to stage a world's fair in honor of the United States Centennial. He passed his suggestion along to the mayor of Philadelphia and the idea began to be kicked around. Detractors thought it would cost too much money and other countries would not be interested but the Centennial International Exhibition of 1876, the first official World's Fair in the United States, was a huge success. More than 14,000 businesses participated, almost ten million visitors passed through the turnstiles in Fairmount Park and modern marvels like the telephone were unveiled to the world. Philadelphia had learned how to celebrate Independence Day.

In 1976 America's Bicentennial got dispersed to events across the country but in the early 1990s the City hit on a formula to insure that Americans would equate independence with Philadelphia - the nation's biggest birthday bash with seven days of events leading up to July 4. Welcome America includes concerts by the world famous Philadelphia orchestra and Philly Pops, popular movies featuring Philadelphia, an ice cream festival, the Taste of Philadelphia with samples from eateries around town, an Independence Day Parade and much more. And fireworks, fireworks, fireworks.

Blobfest
Phoenixville - Colonial Theatre
July

The Colonial may be the only theater in America more famous for being in the movies than for showing movies. The first stage show in Harry's Colonial Opera House was held on Saturday, September 5, 1903. Internationally known actor Fred E. Wright starred in the musical extravaganza *The Beauty Doctor*. The first movie presentation, a series of four one-reelers lasting 40 minutes, was shown on Saturday, December 19th that year. Harry Houdini appeared in 1917, amazing Phoenixville by freeing himself from inside a burglar-proof safe.

In 1957 a local film company started shooting a very low-budget horror movie about an amorphous man-eating gob of silicone with an unknown actor named "Steven" McQueen in the lead. One scene called for movie patrons to run out of a movie theater in a frenzy to escape the gelatinous terror. That scene was filmed at the Colonial. The movie was *The Blob* and it became a cult classic. Since the marquee proudly announcing the Colonial as "healthfully air conditioned" is clearly visible in the movie the place became an icon for movie buffs.

By the 1990s the Colonial was dark but it dodged the wrecking ball and restoration efforts brought the stage back to its 1950s appearance. A re-creation of the movie house's star turn in *The Blob* with patrons spilling onto Bridge Street was staged each summer ith patrons spilling . That event has now evolved into Blobfest, one of the Delaware Valley's funnest festivals.

Philadelphia Folk Festival
Schwenksville - Old Pool Farm
August

The year was 1962 and the members of the Philadelphia Folksong Society had cobbled together an event highlighted by Ramblin' Jack Elliott. The organizers were hoping for 70 people to come, 100 tops. Days before the show folk legend Pete Seeger was added to the line-up and the first Philadelphia Folk Festival wound up with 700 attendees. Each performer was paid $150. Seeger returned his check with a note that read, "Use it to put on next year's event."

More than a half-century later the Philadelphia Folk Festival is the longest continuously running outdoor musical festival of its kind in the United States. Staged over four days with 75 hours of music on six stages, the acts span the range of traditional and roots music. During the weekend some 5000 festival-goers set up camp in the woods of Old Pool Farm, creating a village atmosphere rife with impromptu performances and singalongs. A major part of the festival is the traditional craft vendors who give demonstrations all weekend long.

Revolutionary Germantown Festival
first Saturday in October

Although Philadelphia is the city most associated with the American Revolution, the fighting here took place with words and not muskets. The only major clash of the two armies within the borders  of Philadelphia occurred in Germantown on a foggy October morning in 1777. General George Washington launched an audacious strike in four waves designed to dislodge the British from the Colonial capital. Spirited fighting centered around Cliveden, a grey stone building that served as the home of chief justice of Pennsylvania, Benjamin Chew. The commemoration of the Battle of Germantown is marked each year by events at historical landmarks up and down Germantown Avenue. Costumed soldiers reenact the battle on the Cliveden grounds while actors portray recognizable American patriots. Hint: if you want to back the winning side, wear your redcoat.

Terror Behind the Walls
Eastern State Penitentiary
Halloween

There is no more appropriate place to celebrate Halloween in Philly than Eastern State Penitentiary, the most famous prison in the world after it was built in 1829. Author and social commentator Charles Dickens traveled from England just to see its revolutionary wheel-like design with rows of cellblocks radiating from a central yard. Eastern State Penitentiary was the largest and most expensive public building America had ever seen, capable of keeping 300 prisoners under lock and key in solitary confinement. Each cell had a faucet to supply running water and eventually a flush toilet as well. The so-called humane conditions were labeled the "Pennsylvania System" and an estimated

300 prisons on four continents were built on Eastern's blueprint, leading many to call it America's most influential building.

Eastern State operated until 1970 and then sat crumbling into decay in a state of "preserved ruin." For a quarter-century there were no efforts at restoration or even maintenance. In 1991 the old prison was used as a Halloween fundraiser and it was quickly apparent that Philadelphia was sitting on a vast, untapped entertainment resource. Today the penitentiary is open for tours seven days a week and Eastern State rests comfortably near the top of every Philadelphia travel itinerary.

And that Halloween event that started it all gets darker and scarier each year. Terror Behind the Walls employs Hollywood-quality special effects to simulate a riot inside Cellblock 12, a 3-D fun house and a pitch-black tour of the prison block. Over 200 performers are abetted by digital sound, animatronic creatures and gruesome props to create one of America's most frightening experiences.

A Longwood Christmas
Kennett Square - Longwood Gardens
late November to mid-January

One of the world's great public gardens traces its beginnings to 1700 when George Peirce bought some land from William Penn to start a working farm. Although of modest means the Peirce family nurtured a small 15-acre arboretum for generations with specimens obtained from around the world. By 1850 Peirce's Park was nationally known for its tree collection. But after that the Peirces lost interest in their historic groves and in 1906 an agreement was reached to harvest the farm's timber. Instead Pierre S. du Pont, who was in the process of transforming his family gunpowder business into a modern chemical corporation, bought the property to preserve the arboreal landscape.

Over the years du Pont added his own horticultural wonders to the grounds that expanded to more than 1,000 acres.

The drive out to Chester County to see the Christmas displays at Longwood has been a Delaware Valley tradition since the gardens  opened to the public in the 1950s. By 1984 there were 81 trees adorned with 60,000 lights. Today the grounds are illuminated with more than a half million twinkling lights and inside the four-acre glass conservatory are 18-foot decorated trees interspersed with thousands of poinsettias. The Christmas lights are turned on at 3:30 each day during the season.

Christmas Light Show
Macy's
Thanksgiving to New Year's

Department store pioneer John Wanamaker opened his first men's emporium in his hometown of Philadelphia in 1861 at the age of 23. Wanamaker would build an empire on his then-revolutionary principle: "One price and goods returnable." The present landmark building, at 1300 Market Street, is an Italian Renaissance palazzo of limestone and granite, opened in 1911. Inside, on the second level overlooking a five-story atrium, is the department store's legendary pipe organ, 30,000 pipes strong - America's largest. How important was the opening of this new John Wanamaker's store? President William Howard Taft was on hand for the grand opening. Picture Barack Obama cutting the ribbon at a new Walmart.

Holidays were always a big deal at Wanamakers but in 1955 Christmas became truly magical. A Yale University theater lighting graduate named Frederick Yost transformed the Grand Court into a must-see holiday tradition. His *Magic Christmas Tree* had 85 individual branches illuminated with 23,500 lights, many custom-tinted just for the Show. Another 29,000 lights created figures that blinked to life in the background. A *Dancing Waters Enchanted Fountain* system circulated 3000 gallons of water out front. The entire production was orchestrated from the "Frosty Central" Control Center.

Wanamakers is no more but the store's new overlord, Macy's, has continued the Light Show tradition. Macy's has also acquired and displays a popular Dickens Christmas Village from another legendary mothballed Philadelphia retailer, Strawbridge & Clothier. The third great defunct family retailing empire that once operated in town, Lit Brothers, offered holiday revelers a Colonial Christmas Village; it was also rescued and is on exhibit at the Please Touch Museum in Fairmount Park so it is still possible to see all three.

Smedley Street Christmas Light Spectacular
2700 block of Smedley Street between 16th, 17th, Moyamensing and Oregon avenues
Christmas Season

When Christmas celebrations fueled by personal fortunes or vast corporate war chests become overwhelming Philadelphians head to South Philly where all the residents of Smedley Street come together to display dazzling, color-shifting lights and bulbous blow-up Santas. The smaller the streets in South Philly, the more elaborate the Christmas decorations.

Cheering in Philadelphia

No fan base in sports has more of a reputation than Philly fans. Philadelphia boo-birds are either the best, most passionate, most knowledgeable fans in the country or the worst, most oafish, most demanding fans in the country. Depending on what side of the ball

you are on. Yes, Philadelphia once had an Eagles Court in the bowels of Veterans Stadium where boisterous fans could be hauled and sentenced before a Philadelphia Municipal Court judge during games. But that was before the team moved into its new digs in Lincoln Financial Field where signs warning against "fighting, taunting or threatening remarks or gestures" hang everywhere. These days undercover police have been known to circulate among the crowd wearing gear from opposing teams to keep order.

And yes, the most tired trope in sports fandom - that Philly fans throw snowballs at Santa Claus - is based on real fact. But that happened over 40 years ago in a snowstorm in Franklin Field at the end of one of the worst seasons in Eagles history and involved a stand-in Santa who had been pulled from the crowd at halftime to replace an AWOL Kris Kringle. Expecting more than an ill-fitting makeshift corduroy suit on a 170-pound Santa with a scruffy beard, the fans were just letting Saint Nick know he needed to step up his game. As it was, the "world-famous" pelting of Santa Claus with snowballs was almost completely forgotten as soon as the second half of the game began. It scarcely received any mention in the Philadelphia papers the next day. But the story snuck into the national media and, shall we say, snowballed into the shorthand description of all Philly sports fans that endures to this day - the town so evil they launch snowballs at Santa Claus. And that was 30 years before anyone had ever heard of the Internet.

When you move to Philadelphia you may on occasion hear your new neighbors grouse about the quality of the local gladiators. Before you decide to serve cheese with that whine, consider this: the baseball team, the Phillies, has lost more games than any professional team in any sport in the world - more than 10,000 and counting. They have won only two championships in a history that is fast approaching 150 years. But at least one of those was in 2008 so most Philadelphians can at least remember what it is like to win it all.

The Eagles have never won a Super Bowl and their last NFL championship was in 1960. On the ice the Flyers won two titles in their first ten years of existence but have not lifted Lord Stanley's Cup since 1975. The 76ers assembled one of the greatest basketball teams ever in 1983 but the memory of that championship has had to sustain Philly fans ever since.

Beyond professional games, Philadelphia is the best amateur sports town in America. College basketball fans worship at the altar of the Palestra, the Cathedral of College Basketball. One of the largest arenas in the world when it was constructed in 1927 for the University of Pennsylvania, the Palestra was an early stadium to not have any pillars separating the fans from the action on the court. Although not all games are played there today the Palestra is still the home of the storied Philadelphia Big 5 (La Salle, Penn, St. Joseph's, Temple and

Villanova), the biggest intracity rivalry in college sports.

College football is dwarfed by the Eagles every day of the year save for one Saturday in December when Philadelphia (most years) hosts the Army-Navy Game. Located roughly halfway between the two service academies, the game has been played in Philly 85 times since the rivalry commenced in 1890. The Army-Navy Game is a spectacle unlike any other and on the bucket list of every serious sports fan. Now that you are here, make plans to go.

Collegiate sports in Philadelphia do not begin and end with football and basketball. The Penn Relays Carnival is the oldest and largest track and field competition in the United States. With 15,000 participants more athletes compete in Franklin Field over a week in April than at any other meet in the world. The Dad Vail Regatta is the largest annual intercollegiate rowing event in the United States with more than 100 schools vying for top honors on the Schuylkill River. "Dad" Vail was Harry Emerson Vail, a Canadian who coached crew at the University of Wisconsin until his death at the age of 69 in 1928; the regatta organizers in 1938 named the trophy for him.

Driving in Philadelphia

As a newcomer to Philadelphia you will spend a lot of time in the early going with Google maps. You will quickly learn that there are route numbers that are important and route numbers to forget. The big one to forget - and put it out of your mind right now - is "76."

Wasn't it sentimental of the good folks at the American Association of State Highway Officials and the U.S. Bureau of Public Roads to number the route that slices through Philadelphia from east to west after the birthdate of America in 1776? Well, actually no. It is merely one of those cosmic coincidences that manifests itself on Philly's roadways. Interstate numbering follows patterns hatched back in the 1920s. Main east-west routes were given numbers ending in zero, with the lowest number in the north. With the coming of the Interstate Highway System in the 1950s the grid was flipped with the low numbers starting in the south.

So the first main road heading west out of Philadelphia, the Lincoln Highway built in 1913, got the route number 30. When the Eisenhower system of limited access highways was devised, Pennsylvania already had its own superhighway - the pioneering Pennsylvania Turnpike that had opened in 1940. So the new national grid essentially skipped Philadelphia, building I-80 west from New York City and I-70 to the south. Logistically the Pennsylvania Turnpike had to receive an interstate number midway between 70 and 80, which meant 76.

So you won't be stepping on anyone's patriotic fervor to ignore "76" in Philadelphia. No one uses it. The Pennsylvania Turnpike is never I-76, it is "The Turnpike" on traffic reports and it is always backed up somewhere for construction. Besides it isn't even I-76 all the way from the Ohio state line to the New Jersey state line. The designation ends at the Valley Forge interchange and becomes I-276 for the last 36 miles. That is because in the 1960s it was decided that I-76 should continue from the Turnpike to the Delaware River through the city of Philadelphia instead of around it using...

...the Schuylkill Expressway. The busiest road in the Commonwealth of Pennsylvania goes by many names - the "Surekill Expressway" or the "Surekill Distressway" thanks to its narrow lanes and left-lane entrances and exits are two - but is seldom referred to as I-76. The rugged terrain and challenging routing of the road has defeated

most efforts at modernization - including the jet-pack of Philadelphia highway engineering, a second deck - since the highway opened in the 1950s. It has been altered enough through the years, however, that when city officials submitted the Schuylkill Expressway for status as a national landmark, the proposal was turned down. One thing to be thankful of as you maneuver through the estimated 135,000 cars approaching Center City each day - the 25 miles of the Schuylkill Expressway are the only stretch of I-76 that is toll-free.

There are two more "76" roads to be aware of in Philadelphia, both connecting highways where you will also rarely encounter the numbers outside of road signage. I-676 is better known as the Vine Street Expressway that links the Schuylkill Expressway with I-95 and the Ben Franklin Bridge before continuing on into New Jersey. I-476 is a bit trickier. It is known locally as the Blue Route, although you won't ever see that name on the roads or on maps. The Blue Route links I-95 and the Pennsylvania Turnpike. The route through Delaware County was on planners' drawing boards as far back as 1929, long before those roads were ever contemplated. Due to agitated and deep-pocketed opposition the road remained nothing more that a colored line on those maps until the 1990s. The ultimate route selected for the "Mid-County Expressway" was the blue one. I-476 continues past the Pennsylvania Turnpike all the way to the Pocono Mountains but it is still known by name not number - the Northeast Extension.

Numbers that matter. I-95 is always I-95. Route 1 is Route 1 north and south of the city but in North Philadelphia it is Roosevelt Boulevard (named for Teddy), that is normally short-handed to "the Boulevard." Insurance reports have long ranked intersections along Roosevelt Boulevard as among the most dangerous in the country.

US 202 is an odd road that begins in Wilmington, Delaware and swings around Philadelphia before making its way 630 miles to Maine. It was once envisioned as a beltway around Philadelphia to be called the "Piedmont Expressway." That never happened although you can see the dream in some stretches as you drive it. Even if you don't settle along the highly congested Route 202 corridor you are likely to learn the road for its connection to the King of Prussia Mall, the largest shopping mall in the United States when measured by leasable retail space.

Delaware River Crossings. The most famous crossing of the Delaware River - or any American river - took place on an icy Christmas night in 1776 when George Washington commanded a fleet of shallow draft Durham boats from the Pennsylvania side to the New Jersey side to surprise Hessian troops in Trenton. The second most famous crossing was executed 150 years later when the world's lon-

gest suspension bridge was completed, making it possible to travel from Philadelphia to New Jersey without a boat for the first time. Designer Paul Phillippe Cret created one of the country's most beautiful bridges, far surpassing the quality of its original name - the Delaware River Port Authority Bridge. In 1956, befitting the grandeur and wonder of the span, it was renamed for Ben Franklin. As for cold hard facts, the length of the main span is 1,750 feet, the full length of the bridge is just short of two miles, the towers are 380 feet high and the drop to the water is 135 feet. Crossing on foot is one of Philly's best walks.

Since the Ben Franklin opened, a squadron of decidedly more utilitarian river crossings have followed. With the routes they carry, they are, from south to north: the Delaware Memorial Bridge (I-295) from New Castle, DE to Pennsville, NJ; the Commodore Barry Bridge (Route 322) from Chester to Bridgeport, NJ; the Walt Whitman Bridge (I-76) from Philadelphia to Gloucester City, NJ; the Ben Franklin Bridge (I-676) from Philadelphia to Camden, NJ; the Betsy Ross Bridge (Route 90) from Philadelphia to Pennsauken, NJ; the Tacony-Palmyra Bridge (Route 73) from Philadelphia to Palmyra; and the Burlington-Bristol Bridge (Route 413) from Bristol to Burlington, NJ.

There are so many bridges they ran out of historical figures to honor and just started using the anchor points. Depending on your travel objective and traffic preferences as a new Philly driver you will certainly find yourself forging your own Delaware River bridge strategies.

Eating in Philadelphia

Your new hometown has more trademark cuisine than any American city; here are just some of the foods and brands that define Philadelphia...

Cheesesteaks

More ink has been spilled in the quest to identify the best Philly cheesesteaks than any other local topic. No city's identity is rolled up with a sandwich like Philly is with its cheesesteaks. Remarkably, given the stakes, there is no debate about the origin story of the steak sandwich.

The year was 1930. Pat Olivieri was pushing hot dogs from a small stand outside the Italian Market in South Philadelphia. Weary of spiced sausages for lunch every day, the hot dog man got some chopped meat from the neighboring butcher shop, piled it onto an Italian roll and buried the meat under grilled onions. A passing cabbie thought the sandwich looked good and ordered one. Several weeks later Pat's King of Steaks was open. The greatest inventions always have the simplest backstories.

A "real" Philly cheesesteak is thinly sliced rib eye smothered in Cheez Whiz, although provolone and American are options. Shop signage devotes as much space to ordering etiquette as to the menu in an attempt to distill the order down to two words - choice of cheese and "wit" or "widout" - with or without onions. Only when you have your two words down should you get in line.

After the necessary pilgrimage to Pat's and Geno's across from each other at 9th Street and Passyunk Avenue (both open 24/7, cash only) you too can join in the never-ending Philadelphia quest for the best cheesesteak in town.

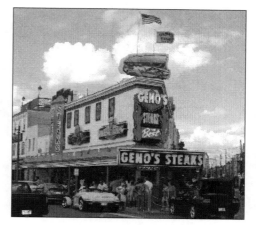

Hoagies

Now that you are in Philadelphia, they are no longer subs, they are hoagies. Hoagies share the same Italian-American pedigree as steak sandwiches but their origin story is as murky as balsamic vinegar. Elongated crusty rolls filled with meats and cheeses began appearing in the early 1900s - up in Maine the "Italian sandwich" is the state's signature sandwich.

In the Philadelphia region the sandwiches gained popularity with workers building warships at Hog Island along the Delaware River. Naturally lunch became the time to enjoy "hoggies." Or maybe the name came from the street vendors who were called "hokey-pokey men." Or maybe the name drifted out of the Italian neighborhoods where those down on their luck were often described as being "on the hoke" while subsisting on scraps doled out by deli owners.

Italian Water Ice

Italian water ice is best explained to non-devotees by what it is not. It is flavored but it is not shaved ice. It does not contain any dairy like sherbet. It is flavored with fruit but is not sorbet. The frozen dessert sprung from southern Europe about the same time as ice cream - in the 1600s - and is made by the same process except the ingredients are frozen while mixing them, giving them a smooth consistency.

After crossing the Atlantic Ocean Italian ice found its biggest fans in Philadelphia where it is called water ice. The town's biggest chain

is Rita's, started by a former firefighter in 1984 and named for his wife. Line up on the First Day of Spring to get your free cup at Rita's - more than 1.5 million cups (cherry and lemon are the biggest sellers) are distributed that day at over 600 stores.

Soft Pretzels

Not all of Philadelphia's favorite eats came courtesy of Italy. Soft pretzels drifted into town from the larger Germanic populations that settled west of the city in today's Pennsylvania Dutch Country. In 1850 Julius Sturgis opened a bread bakery in a brick-and-stone building on Main Street in Lititz. After eleven years Julius stopped baking bread and was operating the first commercial pretzel bakery in America. How that transformation came about is unknown; the popular legend has Sturgis getting his pretzel recipe from a hobo he had invited in for a meal.

Once Philadelphians discovered the salty treats it did not take long before bakers around the city began churning out their own soft pretzels. Today Italian Market ovens fire up in the middle of each night, baking the world's best pretzels to be scooped up before daybreak by foodcart vendors destined for street corners across the city. Every year, Philadelphians eagerly gobble down twelve times the national average in fresh pretzels, salted to perfection.

But wait. The Pennsylvania Dutch have not retreated completely from the soft pretzel wars. Amish markets feature flavored pretzels sweetened with a coating of creamy butter. These confections have been exported across the country in 1,400 Auntie Annie's Pretzel stands. Their first Cinnamon Sugar and Sweet Almond pretzels were sold in a Downingtown Farmer's Market stand in 1988.

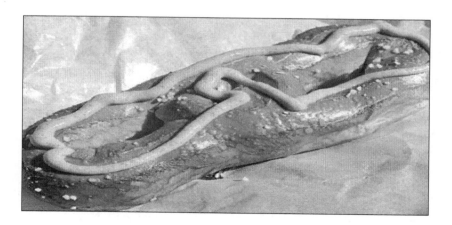

Scrapple

Another legacy to local tables left by the Pennsylvania Dutch settlers is scrapple. The notoriously thrifty farmers were never ones to let anything go to waste and that included the butchering of swine. Offal, your basic head, heart and liver, was boiled into a broth and the fat and bones tossed away. The remaining pig meat was mixed with cornmeal to make a mush which was seasoned with spices and pan fried until a crust formed. It was called scrapple because that's what it was.

In Philadelphia scrapple is typically a breakfast side dish often mashed into fried eggs or laced with horseradish. But the most lowbrow of dishes has been muscling its way onto high-end menus as local chefs re-discover the art of heritage cooking. Fans of the oft-reviled fried pork loaf can test new recipes at the annual Scrapplefest in the Reading Terminal. Or tinker with your own recipes by purchasing some Habbersett Scrapple that is one of America's oldest food brands, having sold the pork product since 1863.

Tastykake

It took a baker from Pittsburgh and an egg salesman from Boston to create the most popular grocery product in Philadelphia history. Small cakes, pre-wrapped fresh at the bakery and sold by local gro-

cers, were a novel idea in 1914 when baker Philip J. Baur and poultryman Herbert T. Morris formed the Tasty Baking Company. The new entrepreneurs sold $28 worth of their Tastykakes on their first day at a dime a cake. By the end of the year they had grossed $300,000.

Tastykakes have been a Philadelphia favorite ever since. The best-selling Butterscotch Krimpet was introduced in 1930 and a few years later Tasty Baking pioneered lunchbox-sized pies. As it approached its 100th birthday the company was baking nearly five million cakes, donuts, cookies, and pies each day. But the Tasty Baking Company never got a chance to celebrate its centennial. Financial difficulties torpedoed the business and forced the shuttering of their landmark Hunting Park Avenue bakery in 2010 and the next year Tasty Baking was folded into Flowers Foods, based in Georgia. The Tastykake brand was not scuttled, however, and its more than 100 varieties of snacks trundles on, still found on their familiar spot on shelves throughout the Delaware Valley.

The quickest way to be accused of being a Philadelphian is to nonchalantly take your package of Tastykakes, flip it over and rub the icing side against your clothes. This will insure the icing on your Juniors, Cupcakes and Krimpets will not stick to the cellophane when you break them open.

Philadelphia Cream Cheese

Old recipe books tell us that cream cheese was popular in America back in Colonial days. The cheese was meant to be consumed fresh, however, and so it was rarely available beyond the local public house that was supplied by a nearby family farm. One place travelers could count on finding rich cream cheese was around Philadelphia.

It wasn't until the 1870s that a New York dairyman figured out a way to mass produce cream cheese. To promote the new product the marketing men gave it a name they knew would scream "quality" to its customers: Philadelphia Cream Cheese. The brand was sold to the Phenix Cheese Company in 1903 and merged  into Kraft Foods in 1928. It is now the largest selling package cheese in the world and in all its years Philadelphia Brand Cream Cheese has been in America's grocery cases it has never been manufactured here.

Bassett's Ice Cream

The Philadelphia label for quality extended to all sorts of products in the 19th century. One was ice cream. Although there was never

a brand of Philadelphia Ice Cream it was widely acknowledged that the city's confectioners were the finest in the country. One of these was Lewis Dubois Bassett, a Quaker school teacher from Salem, New Jersey who employed mule power to turn his backyard churn beginning in 1861. By 1885 Bassett was selling ice cream on the streets of Philadelphia and when the Reading Terminal Market opened in 1892 the company opened a booth and moved production into the basement. Today Bassett's is still there, the oldest ice cream company in America.

Herr's

Pennsylvanians eat more potato chips than residents of any other state. In 1946, when he was 21 years old, young Jim Herr bought himself a potato chip company in Lancaster. In his early days sales averaged about 30 dollars a week. A decade later Herr's pioneered flavored potato chips and today the company distributes over 340 products in 28 states. You can drive out to see the Chester County plant in operation on weekdays with a free factory tour. You will see more potatoes than you've ever seen before in one place before winding up at the snack bar to nosh on tasty free samples.

Reading Terminal Market

Foodies on the prowl in Philadelphia will always find their way to the Reading Terminal Market, the nation's oldest continuously operating farmers' market, sooner or later. Usually sooner. As if browsing the historic market stands stuffed with fresh meats, unusual spices and fresh-baked Amish goods were not entertainment enough the market also offers live music, guided tours and food festivals. Cuisine from across the globe is available from more than 80 unique merchants.

Philadelphia has had markets since the late 1600s when town officials herded independent farmers and fishermen into an open area by the Delaware River. Today that tradition is carried on at the Reading Terminal that has operated since 1892 because one of the nation's most powerful railroads got tangled up in the produce business.

When the Reading Railroad wanted to come into Philadelphia the only suitable location was already occupied by the venerable Franklin Market. To gain the right to build its grand station the railroad was forced to incorporate the market into its design. Although there are many historic businesses operating in the Market, such as Godshall's Poultry that has been peddling birds since 1916, Bassetts Ice Cream is the only original vendor remaining.

The northwestern corner of the market is devoted to Amish merchants from Lancaster County who bring their farm-fresh products and distinctive prepared dishes to the Market Wednesday through Saturday. In August the Amish community creates a country fair in the city for three days of traditions, foods and crafts. The entertainment includes bluegrass music, a petting zoo and Amish buggy rides. The festival has been held annually since 1989.

More than 100,000 locals and tourists browse the offerings at Reading Terminal Market every week. City officials say that only Independence Hall and the Liberty Bell are bigger tourist attractions - but they don't serve up Amish sticky buns.

9th Street Italian Market

This is the oldest and largest working outdoor market in the United States, a curb market with its beginnings in pushcarts, wagons, and sidewalk stands lined up along the streets. In 1915 the community's leading businessmen, second-generation Italian-Americans mostly, formed the South Ninth Street Business Men's Association to formalize their retail confederation.

Today you can still come to the Italian Market to score fresh pasta and Italian meats and cheeses but you will also find delicacies from vendors representing the more recent immigrant waves into the neighborhood. Even as some of the stands have modernized the market still retains its Old World feel, right down to the fire barrels that burn in the winter to keep shoppers toasty.

Exploring in Philadelphia

Of course as a new Philly resident of you will check off the Museum of Art, the Franklin Institute, the Liberty Bell and the Philadelphia Zoo from your to-do list if you haven't done so already. All the greatest hits. But what about the deep tracks around the City?

Barnes Foundation
2025 Benjamin Franklin Parkway

Albert Barnes was born into a working class Philadelphia family in 1872. To get money for an education at the University of Pennsylvania he tutored, entered prizefights and played semi-professional baseball. He earned a medical degree by the age of 20 and in 1899 he co-developed a drug to treat gonorrhea. Barnes' astute business sense in marketing Argyrol made him rich and he began spending his money on art. He concentrated his buying sprees on the Old Masters, accumulating 69 Cézannes (more than hang in all the museums in Paris), 60 Matisses, 44 Picassos, and 181 Renoirs that represented the largest concentration in the world.

Barnes built a mansion to house his collection in Merion outside Philadelphia. He hung his 2,500 works of art cheek-by-jowl according to his theories on art history. He opened the Barnes Foundation as an educational experience more than a museum in 1925. Upon his death in an auto accident in 1951 Barnes' will stipulated that the collection remain exactly as it was. The public was admitted in 1961- but only 500 visitors were allowed each week. Over the years the Barnes Foundation became regarded as a national treasure, protected by restricted access with a preference given to students.

The Barnes collection grew in estimated value to over $25 billion but maintenance costs were buckling the Foundation. Merion officials refused to allow expanded access in the residential area and after a prolonged legal battle the Foundation was permitted to break the will and move the collection to Center City. A 93,000 square-foot gallery was erected in 2012 and replicates the original galleries created by master assembler Albert Barnes as closely as possible.

Bartram Gardens
54th Street and Lindburgh Boulevard

Within sight of the Philadelphia skyline, but out of sight of most of the city, there is a garden that has been growing for almost 300 years. Quaker farmer John Bartram first tilled the ground at 54th Street and Lindbergh Boulevard in 1728 and today it thrives as America's oldest botanic garden. In an era when most people grew up, lived and died without ever traveling more than 20 miles from one's birth-

place, John Bartram began traveling exhaustively throughout the American colonies collecting plants. Although lacking in formal education he was a keen observer and set out to catalog every native plant in America. John Bartram became the first and most formidable botanist in the United States, writing the first books about the natural world in the Western hemisphere.

Bartram cultivated his garden in an eight-acre plot on the west bank of the Schuylkill River. At first he grew plants that piqued his interest and then populated the beds with specimens harvested from his travels. His hobby soon sprouted into a bustling commercial nursery that would expand over the next two generations of Bartrams, eventually encompassing ten greenhouses, more than 1,400 native plants and 1,000 exotic species.

Today the 45-acre plot has been designated a National Historic Landmark and is operated for public enjoyment by the John Bartram Association in tandem with the City of Philadelphia. The plantings are a heritage collection of native plants grown by the Bartrams between 1728 and 1850, some are direct descendants from that time. The star attraction is a *Franklinia altamaha* tree that Bartlett found growing in a grove on the banks of Georgia's Altamaha River in 1765. He grew the tree from seed and named it after family friend Benjamin Franklin. No Franklinia trees have been found in the wild for 200 years and all those growing today are descended from the Franklinia grown in Bartram's Garden.

Fairmount Water Works/Boathouse Row
640 Water Works Drive

Perched on the banks of the Schuylkill River, the Water Works, built between 1812 and 1815 by Frederick Graff, not only gave the City its water, but its rambling classical architecture and cutting-edge engineering made it a world famous 19th-century tourist attraction. Water was pumped from the river into a reservoir (where the Art Museum now stands) and then distributed through the city via  wooden water mains. Graff was a draftsman on the city's first waterworks built between 1799 and 1801 after which he became superintendent of the Philadelphia Waterworks. He remained at the post for 42 years, becoming America's foremost authority on delivering fresh water to the people.

Graff's dam also tamed the energetic Schuylkill River, drawing rowers to the calmer current and providing space for a wide, mile-and-a-quarter course that still exists today. Boathouse Row, a series of 15 tightly-spaced Victorian buildings that are home to Philadelphia's rowing community, boasts a long honor roll of national and Olympic medalists. The City hosts nearly twice as many regattas as the closest competitor city, Boston.

The picturesque boathouses are simple, roomy and functional. The Undine Barge Club at #13, erected in 1882, was designed by Frank  Furness, America's leading Victorian architect. The clubs, that banded together in 1858 to form the Schuylkill Navy, outline their landmark boathouses with lights at night; they were added in 1979 by famed architectural lighting designer Ray Grenald. Instead of being torn down, as was the plan, Boathouse row emerged as one of Philadelphia's most enduring images.

Mutter Museum
19 South 22nd Street

The College of Physicians traces its roots back to 1787 when 24 Philadelphia doctors banded together to advance the investigation of diseases, especially those that were peculiar to North America. It is the oldest private medical society in existence in the country. The following year the College of Physicians established a medical library which became the cornerstone of subsequent research into the history of medicine in America; the collection boasts over 12,000 rare books, including 400 printed before 1501.

Thomas Dent Mutter was born in Richmond, Virginia in 1811. He earned a medical degree at the University of Pennsylvania at the age of 20 and sailed across the Atlantic Ocean to study under the master surgeons of Europe. Fascinated by cases of deformity, Mutter

developed a specialty in reconstructive surgery. He sailed back to Philadelphia and signed on to the faculty of Jefferson Medical College in 1841.

Ill health forced Mutter to resign his chair of the Principles and Practice of Surgery in 1856 and he died three years later in Charleston, South Carolina at the age of 48. During his lifetime Thomas Mutter assembled a collection of over 1,700 medical curiosities which he willed to the College of Physicians along with $30,000 for maintenance. Jefferson, his employer, would have received the diagnostic treasure trove but the school lacked a fireproof building.

The College of Physicians began displaying the artifacts in 1863 but it was little known outside the medical community for 125 years. In 1988 new museum director Gretchen Worden began taking the Mutter's oddities to the public, including frequent appearances on television with David Letterman; annual attendance leaped from a few hundred to 60,000. Housed in a 1909 Colonial Revival brick-and-limestone building in the city's Rittenhouse Square neighborhood, the Mutter's oft-times macabre collection shows off such treasures as President Grover Cleveland's cancer-riddled jawbone, bullet-shattered bones, and a cast of the original Siamese twins, Chang and Eng Bunker, who lived 63 remarkable years before dying within three hours of each other in 1874.

The Rosenbach Museum and Library
2008 Delancey Street

If there was a hall-of-fame for collectors the Rosenbachs would certainly be in it. Abraham Simon Wolf Rosenbach was the youngest of eight children born into an old Philadelphia family. As a lad, Abraham spent many hours in the antiquarian bookshop of his uncle which set him on a life-long pursuit of collecting.

But Rosenbach saw something in his pursuit of books that many of his contemporaries did not - money. He is considered the pioneer of rare American book-collecting and launched many a library. Rosenbach kept plenty himself, however. In 1947 he ponied up $151,000 for America's only copy of a Bay Psalm Book printed in 1700, the highest price ever paid for a book at that time.

Both Abraham and his older brother Philip, an expert in fine arts and antiques, left their possessions to be shared with the public after their deaths, which occurred in the 1950s.

The 130,000 manuscripts, 30,000 rare books and other artifacts were organized into a museum along with the dark brick, Civil War-era townhouse on Delancey Place the brothers shared for the last 25 years of their lives. Today the house is open for guided tours and features Egyptian statuary, Persian rugs, 18th-century furniture and Thomas Sully paintings that graced the home. A special hands-on tour allows visitors to spend an hour with rare marvels not on view to the public.

Playing in Philadelphia

Philadelphia started America's first public park and Philadelphians have been hard at play ever since...

Parks

Fairmount Park is America's first public park, started with five acres in 1812. Today, it is the largest contiguous landscaped municipal park in the world with more than 9,000 acres and the bucolic home to an estimated 2,500,000 trees. Here you will find the world's first zoo, a bevy of historic houses and Philadelphia's go-to summer concert stages.

Recreation seekers head for the Forbidden Drive that traces a seven-mile journey through the Wissahickon Gorge, so named when it was closed to automobiles in the 1920s. In 1855, a hotel opened on Rex Avenue and to draw attention to his hostelry the proprietor constructed an Indian from old barn boards and propped it up on top of a rock overlooking the Gorge. In 1902, when the Indian Rock Hotel was long gone but with the silhouette still there, artist Massey Rhind was commissioned to make a representation of a "Delaware Indian, looking west to where his people have gone." The kneeling warrior has gazed up the Wissahickon Gorge ever since - you can follow a switchback trail that gets close enough to pat his knee.

Love Park is the brainchild of Philadelphia City Planner Edmund Bacon (father of actor Kevin) and designed by architect Vincent Kling in 1965 as the anchor space for Benjamin Franklin Parkway. It covers an underground parking garage. The main features of the plaza are curved granite steps and a single spout fountain which was

added in 1969. The familiar LOVE sculpture, designed by Robert Indiana, was first placed in the plaza in 1976 as part of the Bicentennial celebration.

Its planners envisioned a passive recreation space but unwittingly created one of America's best skateboarding parks - even if the activity wasn't exactly legal. Skateboarders in the 1990s moved to Philadelphia from all over the world just to navigate LOVE Park's granite ledges and serpentine steps. Thanks to the influence of LOVE Park, Philly hosted ESPN's X Games in 2001 and 2002, the only times the competition was staged outside of California this century.

The skateboarders always butted heads with City Hall next door, however, and eventually the plaza was redesigned with planters, grass and wooden benches to destroy its appeal as an unofficial skateboard dream park. The boarders moved away and the plaza drifted back to its original purpose as a place to sit and have a bite to eat.

Fishing

It may not be the first thing that springs to mind when you come to Philly but you have just moved into a fishing hotspot. The Schuylkill River, laden with 40 species of fish, flows through the center of the City and is convenient to public transportation. Anglers dropping lines on the Schuylkill Banks between Locust and Walnut streets and further downstream at the Grays Ferry Crescent Explanade can expect to land catfish, perch, sunfish, carp and bass.

Out in the Delaware River the American shad swims as undisputed king. In Philadelphia the shad is the piscine equivalent of the Liberty Bell; the abundance of shad hauled from the area rivers are credited with saving starving Continental troops at Valley Forge. The fish were one of the main reasons George Washington was camped there in the first place.

Shad are among the strongest and hardest-fighting of all freshwater fish and its popularity as a trophy game fish. Pan-fried shad is also one of the Delaware Valley's choicest delicacies - annual shad festivals have been staged in river towns for decades to celebrate the return of the migrating fish to the waters of their birth after spending years in the ocean.

Philadelphia is even a haven for fly fishermen who can chase elusive trout in the area's quickstepping streams. The Wissahickon Creek (from the Lenni Lenape for "a stream of yellow color") flows for 23 enticing miles, dropping over 100 feet in altitude in its final seven miles. Out in Chester County the Valley Creek meanders through Valley Forge National Historic Park and some of the prettiest countryside in the region. It is a cold water stream and the trout are natives making this some of the most challenging fly fishing in the Keystone State.

Floating

Philadelphia's waterways lure more than fishermen on a hot summer day. By the time the Delaware River reaches Philadelphia from its sources on the western slopes of New York's Catskills Mountains it is more than a half-mile wide and dredged to a depth of over 40 feet. But about an hour north of the city the Delaware is flowing through Bucks County at a depth of only one to five feet and you can almost toss your car keys across the river from Pennsylvania to New Jersey. At a peaceful 1.5 miles an hour float trips can last several hours; not including time off for a barbecue meal in the middle of the river with The Famous River Hot Dog Man.

The Brandywine River is so often described as 'idyllic" that it seems

to be part of its official name. For much of the year the river runs so shallow that tubers will often have to stand up and walk their tubes if they miss the preferred course. As it twists and turns into Delaware from Pennsylvania the Brandywine is flowing past ancient croplands and under old trees draping across the water, almost touching from bank to bank. Numerous bridges across the Brandywine are used to create float trips of between an hour to four hours.

In New Jersey the Pine Barrens spread across more than 100,000 acres, mostly impenetrable except for a spiderweb of more than 500 miles of unpaved, unmarked sand roads. In the days of the American Revolution the region's bog ore propped up a booming iron industry that churned out much of the weaponry used in the war. The Batsto River that flows through the Pine Barrens east of Philadelphia is stained the color of tea from eons of decaying plant material; its gentle waters ramble so languidly that most of the commercial outfitters only offer kayaks and canoes that can be propelled. But that doesn't stop tubers from using these waters as well - it just may require a bit of arm paddling to make progress on the river.

For those looking for a more stimulating day on the water the Lehigh River roars between Appalachian Mountain ridges on its way to the Delaware River to create some of the most exciting whitewater on the East Coast. Lehigh River outfitters like to emphasize that their waters offer way more rapids than the Delaware River. Four-mile river trips through the Class 1 Whitewater can last as little as two hours down the churning waters of the Lehigh Gorge.

The Shore

In other places it is the beach, in Philadelphia it is the shore. From City Hall it is 62 miles to the Atlantic City boardwalk. In 1850 there were only seven homesteads on Absecon Island. About that time Jonathan Pitney, a prominent physician, and Richard Osborne, a Philadelphia engineer, got the idea that the ocean's salt air might be a healthy alternative to the sooty air of Philadelphia. The entrepreneurs laid track for the Camden-Atlantic City Railroad and on July 5, 1854 the first train chugged onto the island after a 150-minute trip. The Jersey Shore has been  Philadelphia's summer playground ever since. The world's first boardwalk was laid in Atlantic City in 1870; the forward-thinker who proposed creating an eight-foot wide wooden walkway from the beach to the town was named Alexander Boardman. Really.

Politicking in Philadelphia

Philadelphia is among the bluest of cities - Democratic Presidential candidates can expect at least 80% of Philly votes and there has been a Democrat in the mayor's office since 1952. It has not always been so. Historically Philadelphia was the Republican bastion of the country. For six decades no Democrat sniffed City Hall; in 1932 in a landslide for Democratic reformer Franklin Delano Roosevelt Philadelphia went for Herbert Hoover.

It is a completely different story in the Philly suburbs. Most of the suburban voters are registered Republicans but the Grand Old Party can never take their fealty as a given. Or even a probable. The suburbs are a notorious political battleground, known to swing state elections and color Pennsylvania blue or red in Presidential contests. Every four years the fortunes of area sign makers skyrocket as political operatives infiltrate the counties encircling the City. And some years you can forget about watching television without a strong political filter.

Towns Around Town

Mushrooms are the number one cash crop in the Commonwealth of Pennsylvania and it all started with a Quaker farmer named William Swayne. In the 1890s Swayne began growing the first carnations in the United States in his Kennett Square greenhouse using imported European spawn. The region now produces one million pounds of the fleshy fungus every week, enough for the 300-year old town to proclaim itself "The Mushroom Capital of the World." Kennett Square celebrates its fungiculture by dropping an 800-pound steel mushroom on New Year's Eve and every year since 1985 the streets are given over to the Mushroom Festival in fall. At that time tours are given of the long, windowless concrete growing houses where the classic white button mushrooms are cultivated.

Building to See

Hicks-Schmaltz House
120 South Marshall Street
This eclectic house is a show-off in a town of Victorian-era residences, employing a contrasting mix of building materials and architectural elements. Noteworthy details include a slate-hipped roof, conical roof porch, Chinese lattice work on the porch railing and the classical columns supporting the porch roof. This was once the home of a hardware dealer; today it hosts Borough offices.

With an industrial heritage tripping back to Revolutionary War times when a small mill was built on French Creek to forge nails, Phoenixville has the largest registered historic district in Chester County. The foundry's molten metal reminded the manager of the fabled bird that died and rose from its ashes so the iron works and the town were named for the Phoenix. Phoenix Iron and Steel became one of the largest factories in southeast Pennsylvania and by 1881 was producing 30,000 tons of pig iron a year and employing 1,500 men. The blast furnaces have all gone cold but Phoenixville has been in the process of another rebirth; many stores along Bridge Street have retained and spruced up their Victorian facades.

Building to See

The Foundry/Schuylkill River Heritage Center
2 North Main Street

Built in 1882, the brownstone foundry of the Phoenix Iron & Steel Company poured iron castings well into the 1970s. The works became famous for its Phoenix Column, a hollow and circular beam made up of wrought-iron segments that were flanged and riveted together. The Phoenix columns ruled the world of bridge-building until the development of reinforced concrete in the early 20th century. Abandoned after 1987, the building now does duty as the home of the Schuylkill River Heritage Center. Inside, there is a massive wooden cantilever crane still in its original location that is thought to be the last and largest of its kind in the United States. Outside, an arc of trademark Phoenix Columns grace the entrance plaza.

West Chester grew up at the intersection of two Colonial wagon roads, one that went from Philadelphia to Lancaster and one that went from Wilmington to Reading - an ideal location for a tavern. That roadhouse appeared in the 1760s and became known to thirsty wayfarers as Turk's Head Tavern. But there was no industry here, no water to power it, no marketplace. For the better part of fifty years there was no development beyond shouting distance of the little courthouse. West Chester never became much of an industrial town and developed as the governmental, legal, cultural and commercial focal point of its county instead. Much of the downtown remains intact and the entire district is listed on the National Register of Historic Places. In 2001 an exuberant *Philadelphia Inquirer* article gushed that West Chester was "the perfect town" and borough promoters have taken the compliment and run with it ever since.

Building to See

Chester County Courthouse
2 North High Street

In 1682 William Penn established Chester County as one of three original counties in the Pennsylvania Colony and a Court House was constructed in 1724 in Chester near the Delaware River.

Population density and immigrant migration eventually sent the seat of justice inland; between 1784 and 1786 the first courthouse arrived. The current house of justice, the architectural centerpiece of West Chester, was designed by Philadelphia architect Thomas Ustick Walter in the Greek Revival Style and opened officially on Washington's Birthday, 1848. Walter then departed the Delaware Valley for a bigger commission - to design the dome on the United States Capitol.

While industry played the lead role in the development of most of the towns in Pennsylvania Colony, Media was more of a summer resort spot. Thomas Minshall was one of the first to buy land from William Penn, acquiring property south of Philadelphia in 1702. Since it was situated approximately in the center of Delaware County it was called Media. Minshall's property was also on the highest point in the county and its fresh air and rolling hillsides began to attract Philadelphians seeking a respite from the increasingly foul city environment. Since the sale of liquor was verboten in Media from Day One, the Quakers who came on holiday never had to worry about intrusion from boisterous travelers who hustled quickly on down the road in the hunt for a tavern. The tradition of recreation and leisure prevails today in such landmarks as the Media Theatre, a Beaux-Arts structure with Art Deco design elements that opened in August 1927 with a screening of the first talkie, *The Jazz Singer*. Admission was 25 cents. After 75 years as a movie palace the historic space was transformed into the Media Theatre for the Performing Arts in 1994.

Building to See

Delaware County Court House
Front Street at the head of South Street

The original section was completed in 1851 with one courtroom. The structure was later expanded and altered in 1871, 1913 and 1929 to exude a more classical appearance behind Ionic columns; it is generally regarded as one of the handsomest court houses in the eastern United States. William Jennings Bryan once orated from the front steps and Ronald Reagan also spoke here.

In 1784, after Montgomery County was pulled out of Philadelphia County, a 27.5-acre parcel was purchased for the new county's seat of government. It took the name of an ancient landowner in the area, Isaac Norris. Norris had been mayor of Philadelphia 60 years earlier - Ben Franklin had just gotten to town and George Washington wasn't even born yet. Norris may be the oldest person for whom a Pennsylvania town is named. Norristown was not destined to be a sleepy government town, however. Water draining into the Schuylkill River along the Stoney Creek and Saw Mill Run encouraged early industry. The Schuylkill Canal was completed in 1826 and the Reading Railroad arrived in 1834. Norristown had some of the earliest electrified trolley lines in America. It was heady enough for borough boosters to proclaim in its Centennial literature in 1884 that, "Norristown is now the biggest, busiest, brightest Borough in the world."

Building to See

Montgomery County Jail
north side of East Airy Street between Church Street and DeKalb Street

The prison was constructed in 1853, as part of the same plan that created the Greek Revival-style Court House. Each was designed by Napoleon LeBrun, who provided versions of both buildings in both Gothic Revival and classical styles. The non-matching Gothic visage was chosen for the intimidating jail and executed in solid granite. There is an underground tunnel for conveying prisoners to and from the Court House.

John Potts built a Colonial-era iron empire at the confluence of the Schuylkill River and Manatawney Creek in the 1750s. In 1761 he advertised building lots for sale in a new town he was calling Pottsgrove, situated along the Great Road that led from Philadelphia to Reading. The village grew slowly, inhabited mainly by Pottses - John had 13 children. By 1840 there were still less than a thousand people living in the rural village when the new Philadelphia and Reading Railroad made a fateful decision to run its tracks on Pottstown's side of the Schuylkill River and locate much of its car building and repair facilities in the town. The population

would grow 16-fold before the end of the 19th century as Pottstown's heavy industry became known nationwide. Most of the building stock on the present-day streets emanates from the boom days of the late 1800s through early 1900s.

Building to See

Pottsgrove Manor
100 West King Street

Potts began construction of his manor house, one of the finest homes to be built in the region, in 1752. Today it is a go-to example of Georgian architecture in Pennsylvania. Pottsgrove Manor features ashlar walls, pedimented gables and classic five-part symmetry under a cedar roof. Only about four acres of the expansive Potts plantation remain today but fortunately it includes this building, the oldest structure in the borough.

Doylestown is unique among prominent Pennsylvania towns. There is no water here to power industries; not even a mill. There is not a wealth of natural resources nearby. The railroad never rolled through town with the promise of progress. No important school was founded here to attract new residents. The reason Doylestown is here today is because it was the exact spot where the colonial road from the Schuylkill River at Swede's Ford to the Delaware River at Coryell's Ferry crossed the main road linking Philadelphia to Easton. In 20th century automobile-speak, it is where Route 202 crosses Route 611. To a Delaware Valley traveler of the early 1700s, it was simply "the crossroads," a place to meet and arrange transport of their goods; while they waited for the ferrymen they slept in their wagons and hoped for good weather. Doylestown evolved into the professional and residential character it exudes today. Lawyers drawn to the county seat set up shop in existing houses or built new houses that doubled as offices. Even the buildings erected in downtown Doylestown as office buildings often don't look like office buildings.

Building to See

Mercer Museum
84 South Pine Street

Prolific Pulitzer Prize-winning novelist James Michener is Doylestown's favorite son but no man did more for the town, or just about any town in the Delaware Valley, than Henry Chapman Mercer. Born in 1856 into a Bucks County family, Mercer became a leader of the Arts and Crafts movement of the early 20th century. His Moravian Pottery and Tile Works, opened in 1912, produced hand-crafted tiles that adorn buildings throughout the world. In 1916 Mercer erected this utterly unique six-story concrete castle to house his collection of some 40,000 objects that document the lives of everyday early Americans. The towering central atrium was used to hang the largest objects such as a whale boat, stage coach and Conestoga wagon. On each level surrounding the court, smaller exhibits were installed in a warren of alcoves, niches and rooms according to Mercer's classifications - healing arts, tinsmithing, dairying, illumination and so on. Across town on the grounds of his tile works, Mercer's home, Fonthill, is another eccentric masterpiece with 44 rooms and more than 200 windows of varying size and shape.

Bucks County - Newtown

William Penn had plans that extended beyond his dream town of Philadelphia. His grand scheme included satellite towns where city residents could build country homes and establish farms. So in 1682, legend has it, he rode north and stopped in a grove of trees where a creek meandered towards the Delaware River and declared it the spot where he was going to build his "new town." Penn sketched out 16 farm plots that would be connected to a common. Newtown became the seat of government in Bucks County and was an important supply center during the American Revolution. From this location, Washington marched his army into American legend on Christmas Eve to cross the Delaware and surprise a drowsy Hessian camp in Trenton. The county government left for Doylestown in 1813 and Newtown settled into a comfortable residential existence. Gradually the heritage farms gave way to houses and the borough was enlarged four times beginning in 1838. All the while the core of town in Penn's original common resisted the overtures of modernization. The Historic District is listed on the National Register of Historic Places with many of its buildings well into their third century of use.

Structure to See

Centre Avenue Bridge

The stone Centre Avenue Bridge was constructed in 1796; it is the oldest remaining bridge in Bucks County and the fourth oldest in Pennsylvania. The bridge was designed with Roman arches, the height of sophisticated engineering at the time. The workmanship of the stone masons was exemplary. The Centre Avenue Bridge shares a foundation on its western approach with the McMasters House, which was built in 1833.

Bucks County - Bristol

Not all of Pennsylvania Colony was William Penn land. North of Philadelphia, Samuel Clift received a land grant of 262 acres from Governor Edmund Andros of New York in order to start a ferry service across the Delaware River. He was also required to operate a public house on the site. Bristol, the town that grew up around Clift's river shuttle is the third oldest town in Pennsylvania, started in 1681. Primarily populated by Quakers, Bristol rapidly gained importance as a market town and a critical link on the stagecoach route between Philadelphia and New York. In 1832 a 60-mile canal was completed between Easton and Bristol, making the Delaware River navigable for barges floating anthracite coal out of the Pennsylvania mountains and Bristol became the most important industrial town in Bucks

County. Manufactured goods were churned out well into the 1900s but by the time the town celebrated its Tricentennial in 1981 it was ready to turn the page. The canal was decades closed and its lagoon by the Delaware River filled in and converted to a park. A railroad spur into town also was closed and converted into a park. The land that had contained the famous mineral spas was a shopping plaza. As it looked forward to its fourth century, Bristol reached back into its past and created an historic district in its downtown. More than 300 residential and commercial buildings qualified for inclusion, some dating back to the early 18th century.

Building to See

King George II Inn
102 Radcliffe Street, northeast corner of Mill Street

The King George II Inn is the public house established by Samuel Clift in 1681 as the Ferry House; it is considered the longest continuously operated inn in America. After a damaging fire, the hostelry was purchased in 1735 by Charles Besonett who rebuilt it on a much larger scale. When King George II came to power the inn was gratuitously named afer him in 1765. It set the standard for colonial hotels along the main route from New York to Philadelphia, providing refined hospitality, fine refreshments and a warm and friendly atmosphere for the discriminating traveler in the fashion of royal inns throughout England. The name was scuttled during the Revolution and the hostelry was known as the Fountain House where well-to-do guests came to bathe and drink from the nearby "Bristol Springs" which were known for their medicinal qualities. It wasn't until the mid-1900s that the name, King George II Inn, was restored.

Epilogue

Have you got all that? Now go out and be a Philadelphian.

22282452R00038

Made in the USA
Middletown, DE
13 December 2018